BASIC SKILLS

HAL LEONARD STUDENT PIANO LIBRARY

Rhythm Without The Blues

A Comprehensive Rhythm Program for Musicians

Volume 2

TABLE OF CONTENTS

ISBN 978-0-6340-8804-9

HAL•LEONARD®
CORPORATION

7777 W. BLUEMOUND RD. P.O. BOX 13819 MILWAUKEE, WI 53213

Copyright © 2008 by HAL LEONARD CORPORATION
International Copyright Secured   All Rights Reserved

For all works contained herein:
Unauthorized copying, arranging, adapting, recording or public performance is an infringement of copyright.
Infringers are liable under the law.

Visit Hal Leonard Online at
www.halleonard.com

A Note to Students

Welcome to *Rhythm Without the Blues* – Volume Two. This unique program will take you from the very basics of rhythm to an advanced level of comprehension and performance ability. The materials in your workbook, combined with practice exercises and demonstrations on the CD, work together to bring a clear understanding of the basics of rhythm. The demonstrations, exercises, and dictations will give you the necessary practice so that you will be equipped to understand and perform a vast array of rhythmic patterns.

You will find this series easy to use. This series will require a metronome and a CD player.

Each chapter is divided into smaller sections. This allows you to work at one section for a short period of time. Working in small sections is more valuable than trying to cover large amounts of material. Learning this way lays a good foundation as you continue to build your skills.

All exercises and dictations may be used repeatedly for additional practice or review. For written exercises, you may either erase your answers or use a separate sheet of paper.

YOUR CD:

- You may access tracks on your CD by moving from smaller numbers up or from larger numbers down. Simply press the track buttons to find the desired track number.

▶▶| • This button will move forward through the CD.

|◀◀ • This button will move backward through the CD.

- The dictations and exercises are played once. Repeat tracks as many times as necessary to complete each exercise.

YOUR WORKBOOK:

METRONOME: This program requires the use of a metronome, so let's discuss this first.

In 1816, a man by the name of Maelzel manufactured a mechanical device which sounded an adjustable number of beats per minute. Whenever a composer wants the speed or tempo of their piece to be fixed at a certain number of beats per minute—let's say 60, for example—they will write "M.M." plus the symbol for a note equals 60, just as you see in the box below. The "M.M." stands for Maelzel's Metronome. The number 60 simply indicates that the metronome will beat 60 times per minute. In your workbook, the symbol for the metronome is shown as a bell, as seen below.

> Metronome speed is indicated like this:
>
> 🔔 **M.M. ♩ = 60**
>
> This is how it will be shown throughout this series.

Take some time to consult the manual for your metronome and familiarize yourself with its operation and how it sounds at different settings.

The metronome sound is given to help you establish a standard by which to judge the rhythmic pattern. Each bell represents one pulse or beat of the metronome.

On the CD, you will hear the metronome give a count-off before every exercise or dictation. This will prepare you for the beginning of the exercise or dictation.

NOTATION

You will notice that only the stems of the notes are being used, as indicated below:

Noteheads will only be shown when they are needed to indicate the time value of the rhythm. This will become clear as you progress through the book.

HEADINGS

All of the chapters are set up in the same way. Headings appear on the left-hand side of the page, which introduce a series of tasks designed to familiarize you with various rhythmic patterns.

NEW ELEMENT

Under this heading, you will see a large subdivided table. The first section of the table, **Rhythm**, shows what the rhythm symbol looks like. The second section, **Term**, gives the technical name. The third section, **Value**, tells how many beats that rhythm is worth. In the last section, **Rhythm Name**, a spoken syllable is assigned to that rhythm. See **NEW ELEMENT** p. 9 for an example.

LISTENING

Under this heading, you will be given an opportunity to listen to what the rhythm sounds like on the CD. In the example, you will hear two sounds: (1) the metronome and (2) an instrument sounding the rhythmic pattern on a single pitch.

The example will be demonstrated first. You will then have a chance to practice tapping the example. To tap rhythms, strike the tips of your fingers on the edge of a table, palm facing down. Following this, a musical example containing the new element will usually be heard. See **LISTENING** p. 9 for an example.

TAPPING

Material under this heading presents you with an opportunity to practice the new element without the CD.

You will use your metronome to help keep a steady beat. The metronome marking is indicated beside the heading. Set your metronome to the tempo shown.

You will want to learn to feel the basic beat by tapping it yourself. Begin tapping an even beat, equivalent to the metronome, with the hand opposite the one with which you will be tapping the rhythmic patterns. If you are right-handed, you will probably be tapping the rhythms with your right hand and the metronome beat with your left hand. When you have established a steady beat with one hand, begin tapping the rhythmic patterns with the other hand. At first it might feel like rubbing your head and patting your stomach at the same time, but as you persevere, it will become more and more natural for you. See **TAPPING** p. 10 for an example.

MATCHING

Under this heading, you will see a series of boxes containing rhythmic patterns. Here you will match the patterns you hear on the CD, in correct sequence, by indicating the corresponding letters in the spaces provided. Note that most of the rhythms played on the CD consist of a combination of more than one of the boxes given. See **MATCHING** p. 10 for an example.

DICTATION

The next heading contains a series of exercises in which you will write down the rhythmic patterns that you hear.

Only the stems of rhythmic patterns will be used. This is a form of rhythmic shorthand which will help as you write the dictations. Develop your own shorthand in dictations. For example, if you need to write a series of notes that are joined at the top, simply write the basic outline and fill in the rest later. This will become easier as you progress.

On the CD, you will hear each dictation once. Repeat the tracks as often as necessary to complete each exercise.

- First, listen and tap along with the metronome. Listen closely for the rhythmic pattern associated with each beat.

- Speak the rhythm name associated with each pattern, for example, *ti-ti* or *ta*. You may want to do this more than once.

- Next, begin to fill in the patterns under the metronome symbols using the rhythmic shorthand. Write in as many patterns as you can remember each time.

See **DICTATION** p. 11 for an example.

Remember, with the exercises and dictations, it is accuracy that counts. Speed will come later.

You and your teacher may want to chart your progress. Try keeping a log showing the number of times you had to listen to the exercises before completing them and how accurately you were able to tap exercises the first time.

We recommend that you use the companion series:

Ear Without Fear

Ear Without Fear is a comprehensive ear-training program. Using these two series together will help you to successfully master the dictations and exercises in Levels 3 and 4.

A Note to Teachers

Rhythm Without the Blues is an innovative program aimed at building a clear understanding of rhythm and the ability to perform it accurately.

Rhythm is a complex task that is mathematical in structure. It is distinct from ear training, which has a melodic component and employs different neurological pathways, yet both elements are invariably placed together in music training. The result is often frustration and a sense of failure. Ultimately, these elements will be combined. Levels 3 and 4 provide exercises that integrate rhythmic and melodic components.

We have carefully chosen and organized the materials in this book to make the learning process as accessible to students as possible. The Workbook and the CD are integrated to provide several learning approaches: AURAL, VISUAL, and PRACTICAL. Together, they present a comprehensive, step-by-step learning program for which the student can assume primary responsibility.

The following concepts will be covered in Level 2:

- Note and rest recognition

- Time signatures $\frac{6}{8}$, $\frac{4}{4}$ and **C**

- Note and rest groupings in the time signatures

- Demonstrations, exercises, and dictations covering these areas

Stems will be used to indicate time values. Noteheads are not used unless the notehead indicates the value of that rhythm. This enables the student to focus solely on the rhythmic elements. Rhythm names will be used to facilitate recognition of rhythmic elements. The rhythm names used have been adapted from those developed and advanced by Emile-Joseph Chevé, John Curwen, Zoltán Kodály, and Pierre Perron.

Here is why teachers are finding this series an invaluable aid in the studio and classroom:

- It provides a prepared curriculum.

- Students can work independently with well-formatted, easily understood materials.

- Chapters are easily subdivided for appropriately-sized weekly assignments.

- Exercises and dictations are readily available for weekly testing and instruction.

- Lesson time is maximized for instrument instruction, while ensuring the student is honing musicianship skills.

Students often find the development of essential rhythmic and aural skills less exciting than learning an instrument, so a reward system may be helpful. Consider implementing one, using some of the following suggestions:

- Encourage students to keep a log, outlining the number of sections and exercises completed over the week. They may also want to keep track of how long it takes to complete each exercise. Students' confidence will grow as they begin to see an increase in proficiency and speed.

- Award incentive points for successful completion of sections and increased proficiency. Give prizes and awards based on accumulated points.

It is recommended that students also use the companion series:

Ear Without Fear

Ear Without Fear is a comprehensive ear-training program that works in tandem with *Rhythm Without the Blues*. Using them together will greatly enhance the ability of the student to successfully master the dictations and exercises contained in each series.

CHAPTER 1

Two sixteenth notes–eighth note:

NEW ELEMENT

Rhythm	Term	Value	Rhythm Name
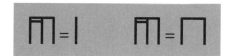	two sixteenths, one eighth	one beat	tika-ti

In *Rhythm Without the Blues – Volume 1*, we learned the *ti-tika*. Our new element, *tika-ti*, is the reverse of *ti-tika*. Two sixteenth notes and one eighth note have a combined value of one quarter note. When this rhythm is tapped it will feel like "short-short-long."

LISTENING

 PLAY CD TRACK 1

 PLAY CD TRACK 2

The following tune contains a good example of *tika-ti*.

9

TAPPING

🔔 M.M. ♩ = 60

For each of the following exercises, tap the rhythm pattern with one hand and the metronome beat with the opposite hand.

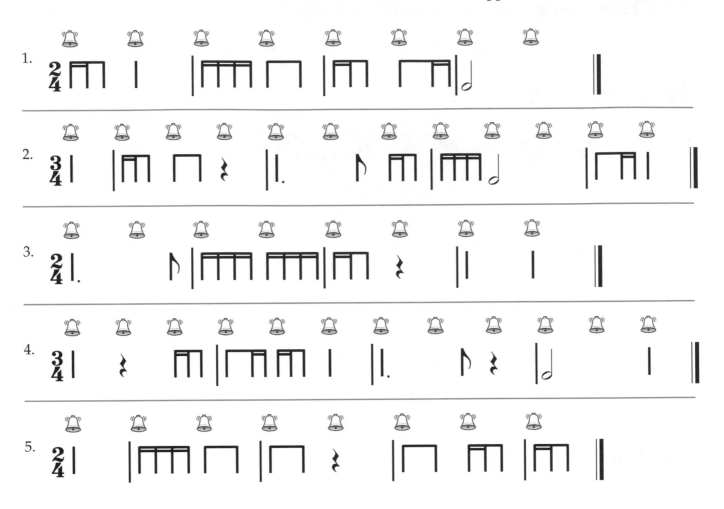

MATCHING

Using the rhythm boxes below, find the rhythms that match the exercises on CD tracks 3–6 and 7–10. Each exercise consists of more than one rhythm box and is played once on the CD. Note that when there is a pick-up measure, the metronome sounds the missing beat(s) before the exercise begins. Write your answers in the spaces provided. Answers are on page 44.

 PLAY CD TRACKS 3–6

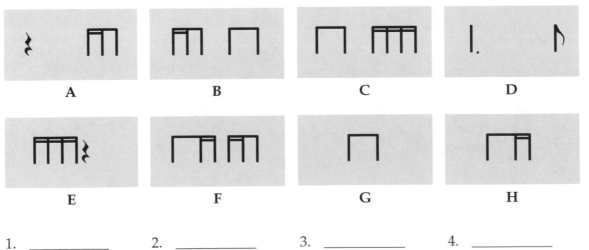

1. _____   2. _____   3. _____   4. _____

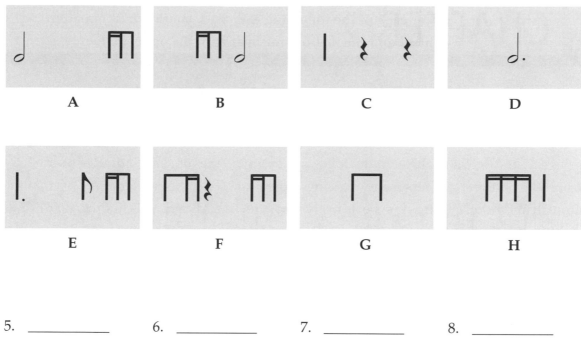

5. _____ 6. _____ 7. _____ 8. _____

DICTATION

Play the tracks one at a time. Under the given metronome symbols, write the rhythm pattern that you hear. Note that when there is a pick-up measure, the metronome sounds the missing beats before the exercise begins. Each exercise is played twice. Repeat the track as many times as necessary. Answers are on page 44.

PLAY CD TRACKS 11–14

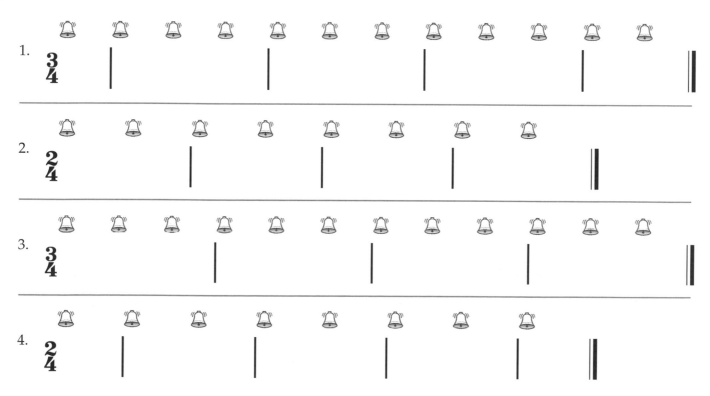

CHAPTER 2

$\frac{4}{4}$ and **C** time signatures, and the half rest: –

We now have a new time signature. In the following example, the top " **4** " indicates four beats per measure and the bottom " **4** " represents a quarter-note beat. This time signature means that there will be the equivalent of four quarter-note beats every measure. In addition, $\frac{4}{4}$ is known as COMMON TIME since it is the most common of all time signatures.

Because of this, it is often indicated simply with a "**C**."

Another way to think of it is like this: $\frac{4}{\rlap{/}4}$

As in $\frac{2}{4}$ and $\frac{3}{4}$ meter, there is a natural accent or emphasis on the first beat of each measure.
The beat emphasis is as follows: strong, weak, medium, weak.

LISTENING

 PLAY CD TRACK 15

Notice that the first metronome beat of each measure has a strong tone.

 PLAY CD TRACK 16

The "Allegro" from Mozart's *Eine Kleine Nachtmusik* contains a fine example of $\frac{4}{4}$ meter.

NEW ELEMENT

Let's look at two new elements, both of which are equal to four beats in **C** or $\frac{4}{4}$ meter.

Rhythm	Term	Value	Rhythm Name
▬	half rest	two beats	re-est

A half rest has the same value as a half note. This rest will never occur in $\frac{2}{4}$ meter. A different rest is used for an entire measure of silence which will be introduced in Chapter 3.

LISTENING

PLAY CD TRACK 17

re - est

In this series, half rests are not used in $\frac{3}{4}$ meter. Two consecutive beats of silence

in $\frac{3}{4}$ are indicated by two quarter rests instead of a half rest.

Some examples of this are included in the following Tapping exercises.

TAPPING

 M.M. ♩ = 60

For each of the following exercises, tap the rhythm pattern with one hand and the metronome beat with the opposite hand.

When tapping and speaking the rhythm names, be sure to turn your hand "palm up" and use "rest, rest" when indicating two quarter rests, and "re-est" when indicating a half rest.

1.

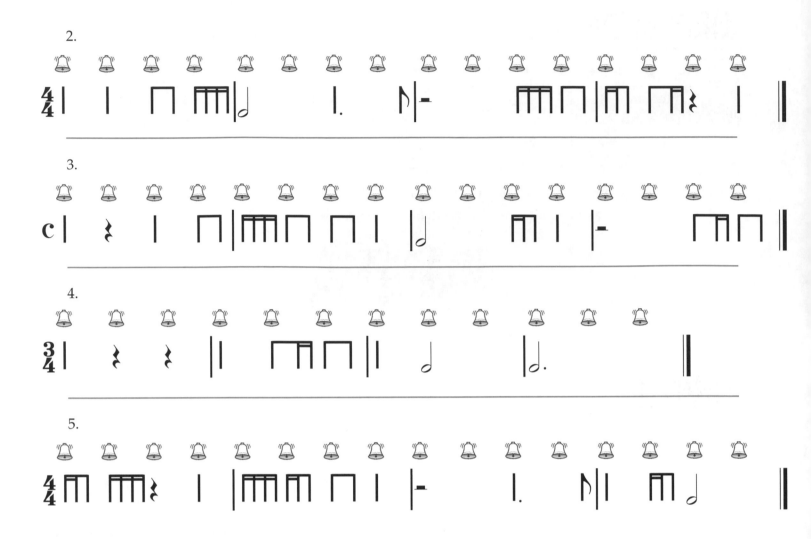

MATCHING

Match the rhythm boxes shown below with the corresponding exercises on the CD. Mark your answers in the spaces provided. Remember to repeat the tracks as many times as necessary. Answers are on page 44.

 PLAY CD TRACKS 18–21

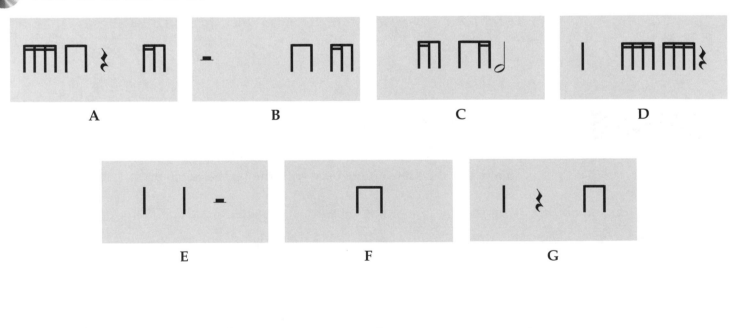

DICTATION

Play the tracks one at a time. Under the given metronome symbols, write the rhythm pattern that you hear. Each exercise is played twice. Repeat the track as many times as necessary. Answers are on page 44.

 PLAY CD TRACKS 22–25

1.

$\frac{4}{4}$

2.

C

3.

$\frac{4}{4}$

4.

C

CHAPTER 3

The whole note and whole rest: o, ‑

NEW ELEMENT

Rhythm	Term	Value	Rhythm Name
o	whole note	four beats	ta-a-a-a

The *ta-a-a-a* symbol is a large notehead without a stem and has a value of four beats. A whole note is held (or sustained) for four beats.

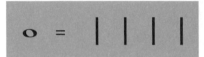

LISTENING

 PLAY CD TRACK 26

ta - a - a - a - a

NEW ELEMENT

Rhythm	Term	Value	Rhythm Name
‑	whole rest	four beats	re-e-e-est

The symbol for the whole rest is an upside-down version of the half rest and has a value of four beats. A whole rest is also used to indicate an entire measure of rest in any time signature. For example, in $\frac{2}{4}$ there are only two beats per measure. Although it may seem that a half rest should be used to indicate a full measure of rest in $\frac{2}{4}$, the musical rule is:

> In any given time signature, a full measure of rest
> is *always* indicated by a whole rest.

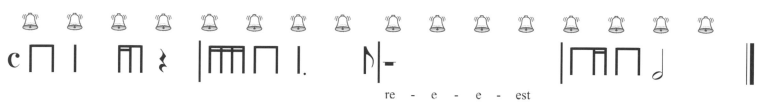

LISTENING

In the following exercise, the whole rest is observed for the equivalent of four beats. The hand keeping the basic beat or metronome beat will continue while the hand tapping the rhythm remains "palm up" for the four counts.

 PLAY CD TRACK 27

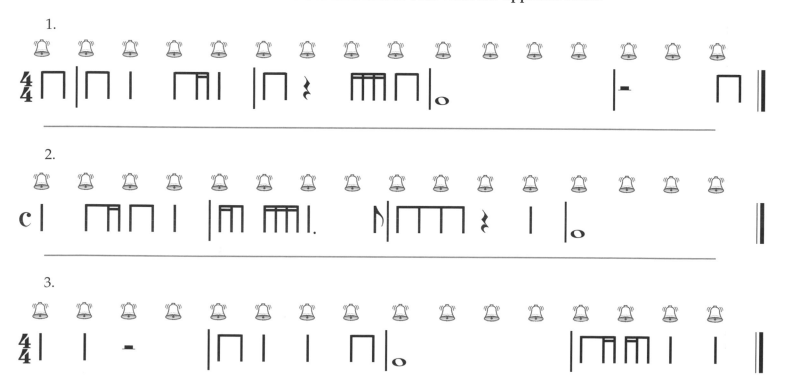

TAPPING

 M.M. ♩ = 60

For each of the following exercises, tap the rhythm pattern with one hand and the metronome beat with the opposite hand.

4.

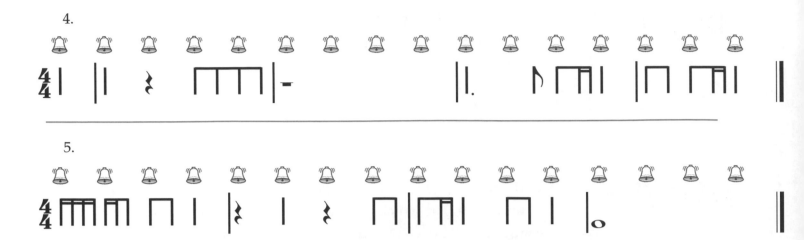

5.

MATCHING

Match the rhythm boxes shown below with the corresponding exercises on the CD. Mark your answers in the spaces provided. Each exercise consists of more than one rhythm box and is played once on the CD. Remember to repeat the tracks as many times as necessary. Answers are on page 44.

PLAY CD TRACKS 28–31

A   B   C   D

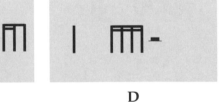

E   F   G

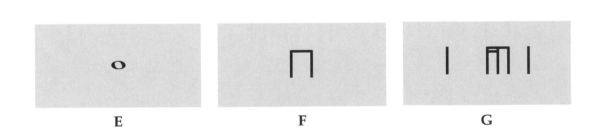

1. _____ 2. _____ 3. _____ 4. _____

DICTATION

Play the tracks one at a time. Under the given metronome symbols, write the rhythm pattern that you hear. Each exercise is played twice. Repeat the track as many times as necessary. Answers are on page 45.

 PLAY CD TRACKS 32–35

1.

2.

3.

4.

CHAPTER 4

The tie

NEW ELEMENT

A **TIE** is a curved line joining two rhythm elements. The value of both elements is combined and the second element does not receive a separate tap.

A tie literally "ties" or joins the rhythm elements together creating one sound. For example, a half note tied to a quarter note sounds like a dotted half note.

In the same way, a quarter note tied to another quarter note sounds like a half.

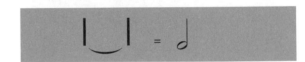

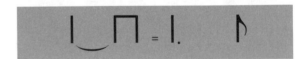

A quarter note tied to two eighth notes sounds like a *tam-ti*.

LISTENING

 PLAY CD TRACK 36

In a melodic line, a tie occurs between notes that are of the same pitch, meaning the same line or space on the staff.

TAPPING

🔔 **M.M. ♩ = 60**

For each of the following exercises, tap the rhythm pattern with one hand and the metronome beat with the opposite hand.

1.

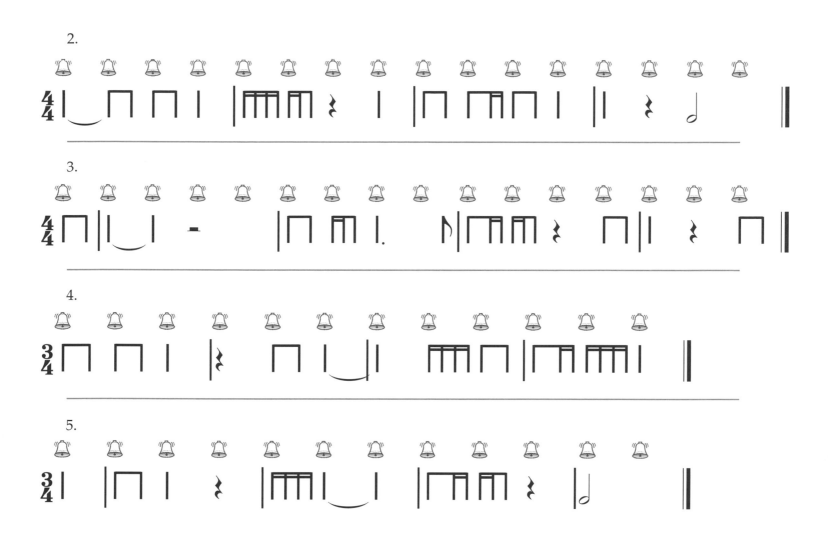

 PLAY CD TRACKS 37–40

MATCHING

Match the rhythm boxes shown below with the corresponding exercises on the CD. Mark your answers in the spaces provided. Each exercise consists of more than one rhythm box and is played once on the CD. Remember to repeat the tracks as many times as necessary.

Answers are on page 45.

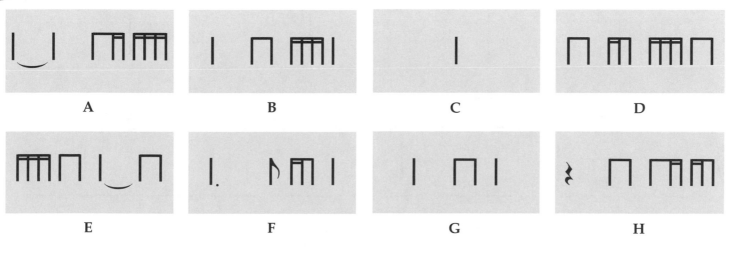

1. _____ 2. _____ 3. _____ 4. _____

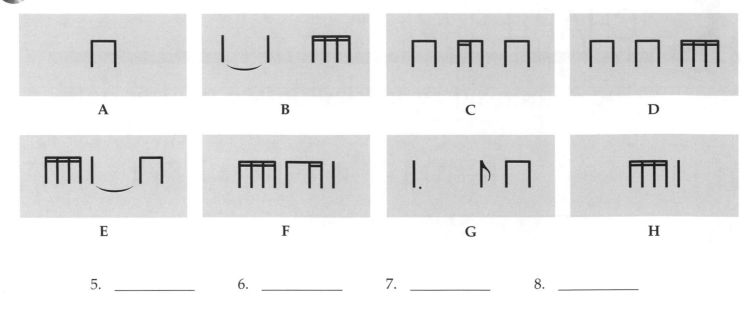

5. _____   6. _____   7. _____   8. _____

DICTATION

Play the tracks one at a time. Under the given metronome symbols, write the rhythm pattern that you hear. Each exercise is played twice. Repeat the track as many times as necessary. Answers are on page 45.

PLAY CD TRACKS 45–48

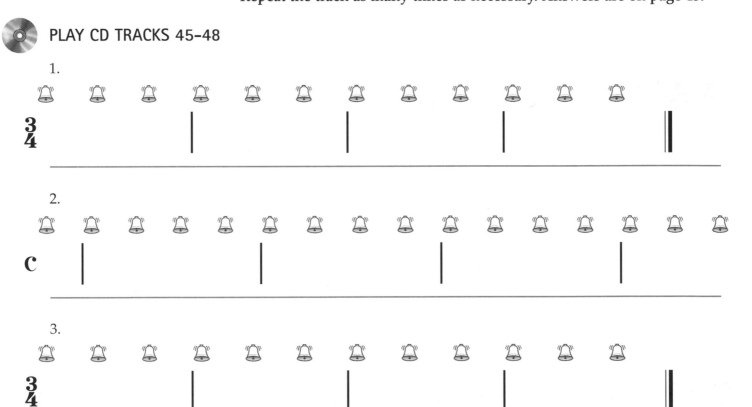

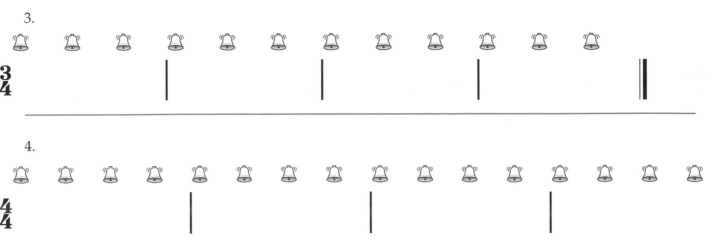

The $\frac{6}{8}$ time signature and dotted quarter note–three eighth notes: ♩., ♫

This chapter will introduce a new time signature. Until now, we have been dealing with $\frac{2}{4}$, $\frac{3}{4}$, and $\frac{4}{4}$ time signatures. These are referred to as SIMPLE METER. Simple time signatures group together (or join with a beam) smaller note values within the quarter-note beat, thus dividing the beat into divisions of two or four.

For example, the quarter-note beat may be divided as follows in $\frac{2}{4}$ or $\frac{3}{4}$ time.

$\frac{2}{4}$	$\frac{3}{4}$

Division by two →

Division by four →

Our new time signature is a type of COMPOUND METER. The main beat in compound time has the value of a dotted quarter note. Compound time signatures group or beam together smaller note values within the main beat in threes or sixes.

For example, the dotted quarter beat may be divided as follows.

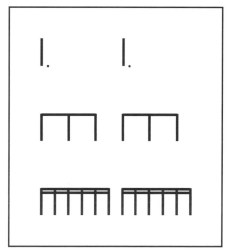

Division by three →

Division by six →

In simple meter, the bottom number of a time signature indicates the value of the main beat. The number "4" in $\frac{2}{4}$, $\frac{3}{4}$, and $\frac{4}{4}$ indicates that the main beat is a quarter note. In compound meter, the main beat is a dotted quarter note, which cannot be represented by one number because it contains a fraction of a beat (one and a half quarter-note beats). However, we cannot show a fraction in a time signature. The next smallest value, the eighth, is used as a point of reference instead.

Using the eighth as a reference point, we end up with a time signature of $\frac{6}{8}$. In the following example the top 6 indicates 6 subdivided beats per measure and the bottom 8 represents an eighth-note beat, which means that there will be the equivalent of six eighth-note beats in every measure. As the example shows, the rhythm elements are arranged in two groups of three eighth-note beats. In other words, there are two main beats equal to a dotted quarter in each measure.

Another way to think of it is like this: $\frac{6}{\text{♩}}$

Notice that the metronome symbols represent a dotted quarter-note beat.

NEW ELEMENT

Rhythm	Term	Value	Rhythm Name
$\natural$	dotted quarter note	one beat	tam

The *tam* symbol is a quarter note followed by a dot. A dot is worth half the value of the rhythm it is placed after, so the dot represents one eighth note. In compound meter, this is equal to one beat.

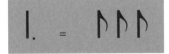

LISTENING

In this example, the traditional counting can help you feel the subdivision of the main beats. Only the rhythm names have been included on the CD.

PLAY CD TRACK 49

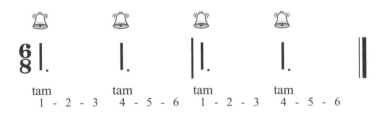

NEW ELEMENT

Rhythm	Term	Value	Rhythm Name
	three eighth notes	one beat	ti-ti-ti

The *ti-ti-ti* symbol is made up of three stems joined at the top with a single beam. This represents three eighth notes. One eighth note is half the value of a quarter note, therefore three eighths are equal to a dotted quarter note.

LISTENING

 PLAY CD TRACK 50

 PLAY CD TRACK 51

The "Gigue" from Bach's *Orchestral Suite #3* provides us with an example of *tam* and *ti-ti-ti*.

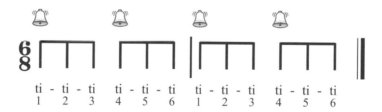

TAPPING

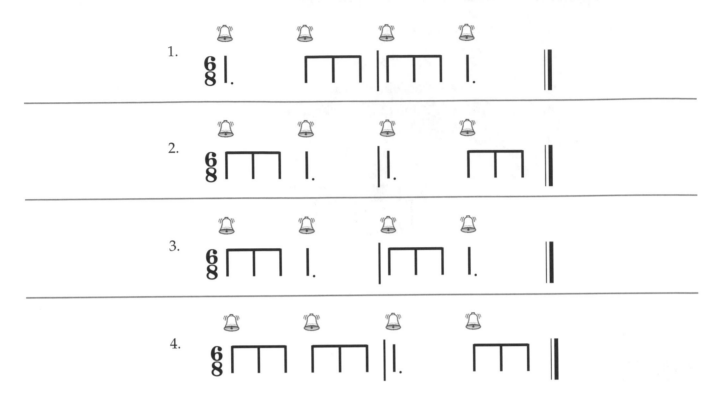

M.M. ♩ = 60

For each of the following exercises, tap the rhythm pattern with one hand and the metronome beat with the opposite hand. Also try tapping while speaking the traditional counting.

MATCHING

Match the rhythm boxes shown below with the corresponding exercises on the CD. Mark your answers in the spaces provided. Each exercise consists of more than one rhythm box and is played once on the CD. All four exercises are on Track 52. Answers are on page 45.

 PLAY CD TRACK 52

A   B   C   D

1. _____   2. _____   3. _____   4. _____

DICTATION

Play the tracks one at a time. Under the given metronome symbols, write the rhythm pattern that you hear. Each exercise is played twice. Repeat the track as many times as necessary. Answers are on page 45.

 PLAY CD TRACKS 53–56

1. $\frac{6}{8}$

2. $\frac{6}{8}$

3. $\frac{6}{8}$

4. $\frac{6}{8}$

CHAPTER 6

The dotted quarter rest: ⸼

NEW ELEMENT

Rhythm	Term	Value	Rhythm Name
⸼	dotted quarter rest	one beat	hush

As we already know, a rest is a beat of silence. The dotted quarter rest has the same value as a dotted quarter note.

$$ ⸼ = ♩. $$

LISTENING

 PLAY CD TRACK 57

TAPPING

🔔 M.M. ♩ = 60

For each of the following exercises, tap the rhythm pattern with one hand and the metronome beat with the opposite hand.

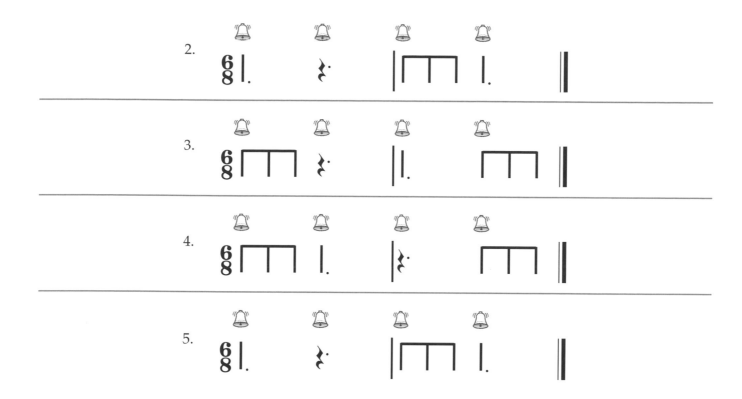

2.

3.

4.

5.

MATCHING

Match the rhythm boxes shown below with the corresponding exercises on the CD. Mark your answers in the spaces provided. Each exercise consists of more than one rhythm box and is played once on the CD. All four exercises are on track 58. Answers are on page 46.

 PLAY CD TRACK 58

A

B

C

D

E

F

1. _____   2. _____   3. _____   4. _____

DICTATION

Play the tracks one at a time. Under the given metronome symbols, write the rhythm pattern that you hear. Each exercise is played twice. Repeat the track as many times as necessary. Answers are on page 46.

 PLAY CD TRACKS 59–62

1.
$\frac{6}{8}$

2.
$\frac{6}{8}$

3.
$\frac{6}{8}$

4.
$\frac{6}{8}$

CHAPTER 7

Quarter note-eighth note: | ♪

NEW ELEMENT

Rhythm	Term	Value	Rhythm Name
| ♪	one quarter note, one eighth note	one beat	ta-ti

The *ta-ti* symbol is made up of one quarter note and one eighth note. These notes have a combined value of a dotted quarter note or one beat in $\frac{6}{8}$ meter.

LISTENING

PLAY CD TRACK 63

PLAY CD TRACK 64

"The Moldau" by Smetana contains a good example of the *ta-ti*.

TAPPING

🔔 M.M. ♩ = 60

For each of the following exercises, tap the rhythm pattern with one hand and the metronome beat with the opposite hand.

1. (rhythm notation in 6/8)

2. (rhythm notation in 6/8)

3. (rhythm notation in 6/8)

4. (rhythm notation in 6/8)

5. (rhythm notation in 6/8)

MATCHING

Match the rhythm boxes shown below with the corresponding exercises on the CD. Mark your answers in the spaces provided. Each exercise consists of more than one rhythm box and is played once on the CD. All four exercises are on track 65. Answers are on page 46.

 PLAY CD TRACK 65

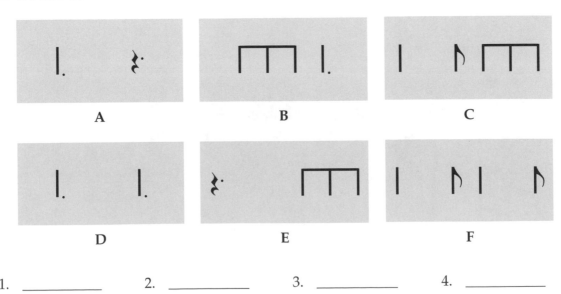

A   B   C

D   E   F

1. _____   2. _____   3. _____   4. _____

DICTATION

Play the tracks one at a time. Under the given metronome symbols, write the rhythm pattern that you hear. Each exercise is played twice. Repeat the track as many times as necessary. Answers are on page 46.

 PLAY CD TRACKS 66–69

1. $\frac{6}{8}$

2. $\frac{6}{8}$

3. $\frac{6}{8}$

4. $\frac{6}{8}$

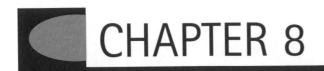

CHAPTER 8

Dotted eighth note-sixteenth note-eighth note:

NEW ELEMENT

Rhythm	Term	Value	Rhythm Name
	one dotted eighth note, one sixteenth note, one eighth note	one beat	tim-ka-ti

The *tim-ka-ti* symbol is made up of one dotted eighth note, one sixteenth note, and one eighth note. These have a combined value of a dotted quarter note or one beat in $\frac{6}{8}$ meter.

LISTENING

 PLAY CD TRACK 70

 PLAY CD TRACK 71

In the third movement of Vivaldi's *La Primavera*, we hear a clear demonstration of the *tim-ka-ti*.

It is important in all exercises and dictations to continue to tap the basic beat with the hand opposite the one you use to tap or write the rhythm patterns.

TAPPING

🔔 M.M. ♩ = 60

As in other time signatures, ⁶⁄₈ will also have incomplete measures. In two of the following tapping exercises, you will have an opportunity to practice starting with a pick-up measure.

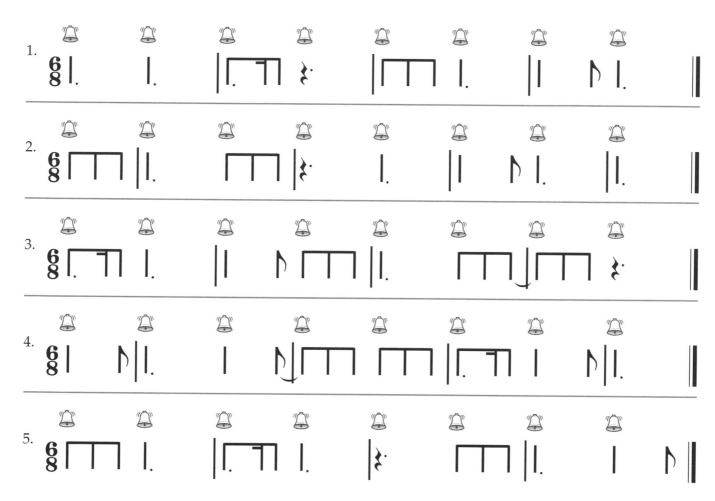

MATCHING

Match the rhythm boxes shown below with the corresponding exercises on the CD. Mark your answers in the spaces provided. Each exercise consists of more than one rhythm box and is played once on the CD. All four exercises are on track 72. Answers are on page 46.

 PLAY CD TRACK 72

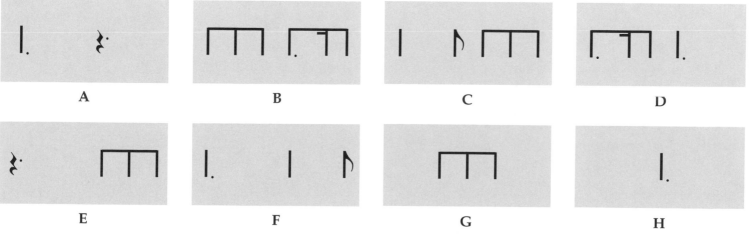

1. _____   2. _____   3. _____   4. _____

DICTATION

Play the tracks one at a time. Under the given metronome symbols, write the rhythm pattern that you hear. Each exercise is played twice. Repeat the track as many times as necessary. Answers are on page 46.

 PLAY CD TRACKS 73–76

1. $\frac{6}{8}$

2. $\frac{6}{8}$

3. $\frac{6}{8}$

4. $\frac{6}{8}$

CHAPTER 9

The dotted half note: 𝅗𝅥.

NEW ELEMENT

Rhythm	Term	Value	Rhythm Name
𝅗𝅥.	dotted half note	two beats	ta-am

The *ta-am* symbol is made up of a half with a dot beside it. This has the combined value of two dotted quarters or two beats in $\frac{6}{8}$ meter.

LISTENING

🔘 PLAY CD TRACK 77

Until now, pick-up measures have had the value of a full beat in the given time signature.
We will now begin to use a partial beat as a pick-up (or anacrusis).

TAPPING

As you can see in the first exercise below, the final measure and the pick-up measure still combine to equal a complete measure in $\frac{6}{8}$ meter.

🔔 M.M. ♩ = 60

For each of the following exercises, tap the rhythm pattern with one hand and the metronome beat with the opposite hand.

1.

(1 2 3 4 5) 6   1   2   3   4   5 (6)

2.

3.

4.

5.

MATCHING

Match the rhythm boxes shown below with the corresponding exercises on the CD. Mark your answers in the spaces provided. Each exercise consists of more than one rhythm box and is played once on the CD. All exercises are on track 78. Answers are on page 47.

 PLAY CD TRACK 78

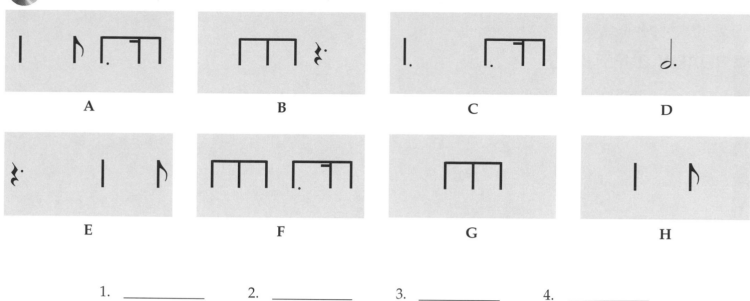

| A | B | C | D |

| E | F | G | H |

1. _____   2. _____   3. _____   4. _____

DICTATION

Play the tracks one at a time. Under the given metronome symbols, write the rhythm pattern that you hear. Each exercise is played twice. Repeat the track as many times as necessary. Answers are on page 47.

 PLAY CD TRACKS 79–82

REVIEW TEST

The number of points for each answer is indicated to the left of each question. This first section has a total of 52 points.

POINTS **REVIEW QUESTIONS**

2   1. Explain the difference between "simple" meter and "compound" meter:_____

_____

1   2. Write the symbol for *re-e-e-est*: _____

2   3. How many basic beats are there in $\frac{6}{8}$ meter? _____ Which rhythm symbol represents this basic beat? _____

1   4. Write the symbol for *tim-ka-ti*: _____

1   5. How many beats would the above symbol receive in $\frac{6}{8}$ meter? _____

2   6. The following symbols appear in $\frac{6}{8}$ meter. Show how they can be subdivided.
     𝅘𝅥. _____   𝅗𝅥. _____

2   7. a) What is the rhythm name for this symbol? 𝅘𝅥 𝅘𝅥𝅮 _____

     b) How many beats would the above symbol receive in $\frac{6}{8}$ meter? _____

3   8. a) How many beats are there in a measure of $\frac{4}{4}$ meter? _____

     b) What is another name and symbol for $\frac{4}{4}$ meter? _____

     _____

2   9. a) What is the rhythm name for this symbol? 𝅝 _____

     b) How many beats does it receive in $\frac{4}{4}$ meter? _____

28

10. Name the following symbols and fill in the number of beats they would receive in the indicated time signatures. Place an "X" if the note or rest would not fit as a complete element in the given time signature. Each blank is worth one point.

Symbol	Rhythm Name	Beats in $\frac{6}{8}$	Beats in $\frac{3}{4}$	Beats in $\frac{4}{4}$
𝅗𝅥.				
♪. ♫				
𝄽.				
𝅝				
▬				
♫				
♩ ♪				

8

11. Write the rhythm names and traditional counting for the following symbols as they would occur in $\frac{6}{8}$ meter. Each blank is worth one point.

$\frac{6}{8}$	𝅗𝅥.	♪ ♩	𝄽.	♫
Traditional counting				
Rhythm name				

52
TOTAL POINTS

YOUR SCORE:_____

Answers are on pages 47–48. If your score is 48 or better,
proceed with the dictations on the following page.
If your score is less than 48, review any areas of weakness before proceeding with the dictations.

DICTATION

Each exercise is played twice on the CD.

 PLAY CD TRACKS 83–94

POINTS

9

1.

$\mathbf{6 \atop 8}$

11

2.

$\mathbf{6 \atop 8}$

9

3.

$\mathbf{4 \atop 4}$

9

4.

$\mathbf{6 \atop 8}$

9

5.

$\mathbf{6 \atop 8}$

9

6.

C

9

7.

$\mathbf{6 \atop 8}$

POINTS

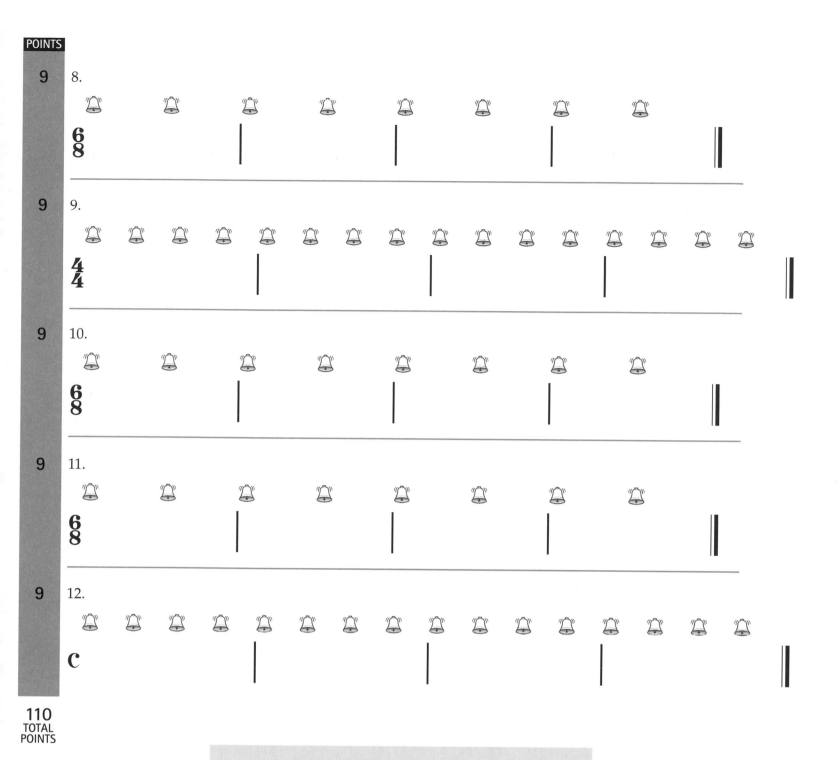

9   8.

9   9.

9   10.

9   11.

9   12.

110 TOTAL POINTS

YOUR SCORE:_____

Each element or note grouping is worth one point, for a total of 110 points.

Answers are on page 48.

If your score is 100 or better, Congratulations! You may now proceed to:

RHYTHM WITHOUT THE BLUES – VOLUME 3

If your score was under 100, review any areas of weakness before proceeding.

Answers

CHAPTER 1

MATCHING:

1. B, D, E, A 　　 2. G, A, C, E, H 　　 3. H, C, F, B, G 　　 4. D, F, A, B

5. B, E, F, B 　　 6. G, C, D, E, H 　　 7. G, E, A, C, H 　　 8. E, B, D, F

DICTATION:

1.

2.

3.

4.

CHAPTER 2

MATCHING:

1. A, D, E, C 　　 2. F, D, A, B, G 　　 3. D, C, B, A 　　 4. F, E, D, C, G

DICTATION:

1.

2.

3.

4.

CHAPTER 3

MATCHING:

1. D, B, C, E 　　 2. B, C, D, A 　　 3. F, B, E, D, G 　　 4. E, A, C, B

DICTATION:

1.

2.

3.

4.

CHAPTER 4

MATCHING:

1. F, A, D, B   2. E, D, F, H   3. C, H, B, D, G   4. A, B, H, D

5. A, D, E, C, H   6. C, B, F, D   7. E, C, G, F   8. G, B, D, C

DICTATION:

1.

2.

3.

4.

CHAPTER 5

MATCHING:

1. A, D   2. B, C   3. C, A   4. D, B

DICTATION:

1.   2.

3.   4.

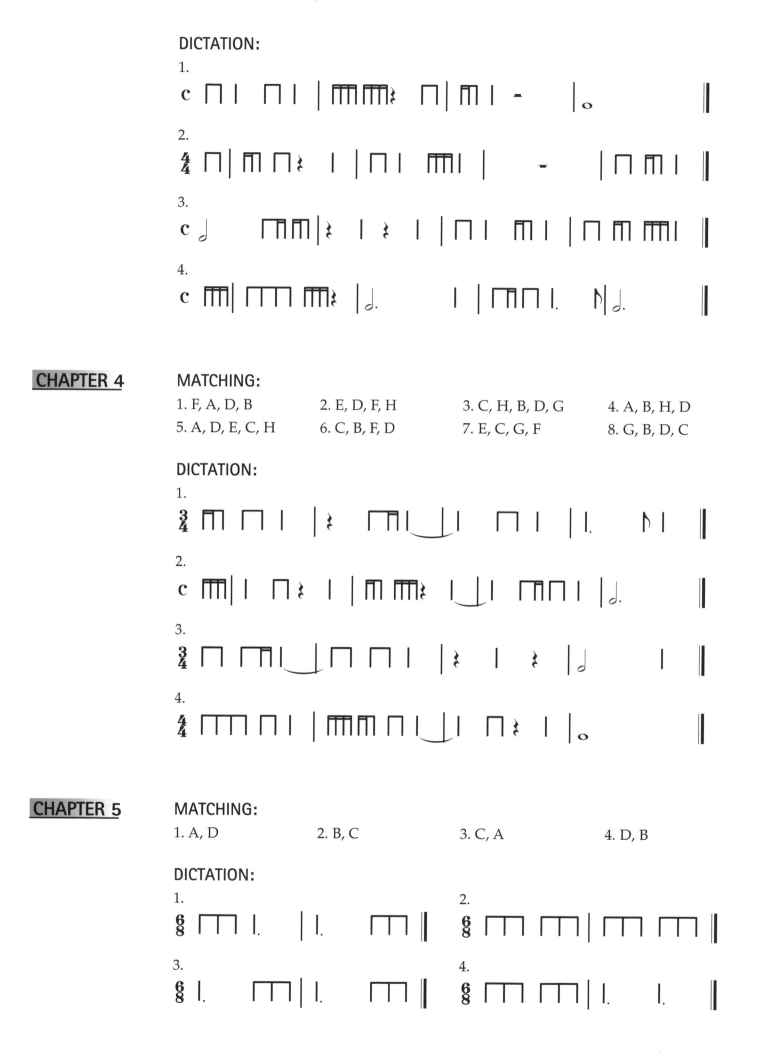

CHAPTER 6

MATCHING:

1. D, F   2. A, E   3. B, F   4. C, A

DICTATION:

1.

2.

3.

4.

CHAPTER 7

MATCHING:

1. A, C, E, F   2. B, D, C, E   3. C, E, A, B   4. F, B, C, D

DICTATION:

1.

2.

3.

4.

CHAPTER 8

MATCHING:

1. C, E, F, C   2. D, B, A, F   3. G, B, E, D, H   4. F, A, B, D

DICTATION:

1.

2.

3.

4.

CHAPTER 9

MATCHING:

1. B, F, A, D   2. G, A, D, E, H   3. H, D, C, B, G   4. C, E, F, A

DICTATION:

1.

2.

3.

4.

REVIEW TEST

REVIEW QUESTIONS

1. In simple meter, the beats are subdivided by two (and four). In compound meter, they are subdivided by three (and six).

2. ▬

3. two, |.

4. ⌐TT⌐

5. one (three subdivided beats)

6. ⌐TT⌐   ⌐TT⌐ ⌐TT⌐

7. a) ta-ti   b) one (three subdivided beats)

8. a) four   b) common time **C**

9. a) ta-a-a-a   b) four

10.

Symbol	Rhythm Name	Beats in $\frac{6}{8}$	Beats in $\frac{3}{4}$	Beats in $\frac{4}{4}$
𝅗𝅥.	ta-am *or* ta-a-a	two	three	three
⌐.TT⌐	tim-ka-ti	one	X	X
𝄽.	hush	one	X	X
o	ta-a-a-a	X	X	four
▬	re-est	X	X	two
⌐TT⌐	ti-ti-ti	one (three subdivided)	X	X
♩ ♪	ta-ti	one	X	X

11.

$\mathbf{^6_8}$	♩.	𝅘𝅥𝅮 𝅘𝅥	𝄽	♫
Traditional counting	1 - 2 - 3 - 4 - 5 - 6	1 2 - 3	1 - 2 - 3	1 2 3
Rhythm name	ta - am	ti - tam	hush	ti - ti - ti

DICTATION:

1.

2.

3.

4.

5.

6.

7.

8.

9.

10.

11.

12.